# The Mystery of the Nativity

# The Mystery of the Nativity

*An Inspirational Drama on the Nativity of Jesus Christ*
*. . . with testimonies from high-profile star witnesses*

Claudette Francis

authorHOUSE®

*AuthorHouse™*
*1663 Liberty Drive*
*Bloomington, IN 47403*
*www.authorhouse.com*
*Phone: 1-800-839-8640*  ← seek an Imprimatur

© *2012 by Claudette Francis. All rights reserved.*

*"The Scripture quotations contained herein are from the New Revised Standard Version Bible: Catholic Edition copyright © 1993 and 1989 by the Division of Christian Education of the National Council of the Churches of Christ in the U.S.A. Used by permission. All rights reserved."*

*No part of this book may be reproduced, stored in a retrieval system, or transmitted by any means without the written permission of the author.*

*Claudette Francis*
*4-170 Brickworks Lane*
*Toronto, Ontario, Canada*
*M6N 5H7*
*Cell: 647 884 INRI (4674)*
*Email: claudettefrncs@yahoo.ca*

*Published by AuthorHouse   10/17/2012*

*ISBN: 978-1-4772-8022-5 (sc)*
*ISBN: 978-1-4772-8021-8 (e)*

*Any people depicted in stock imagery provided by Thinkstock are models, and such images are being used for illustrative purposes only.*
*Certain stock imagery © Thinkstock.*

*This book is printed on acid-free paper.*

*Because of the dynamic nature of the Internet, any web addresses or links contained in this book may have changed since publication and may no longer be valid. The views expressed in this work are solely those of the author and do not necessarily reflect the views of the publisher, and the publisher hereby disclaims any responsibility for them.*

# Contents

Note about this Book ..................................................... 5
Foreword ........................................................................ 7
Author's Acknowledgements ....................................... 9
Introduction ................................................................ 11
Cast of Characters ...................................................... 13

King Herod Defends Himself ..................................... 15
Angels Announce Jesus' Birth .................................... 23
Shepherds Receive the Good News ........................... 29
Joseph, A Man of Integrity ......................................... 35
Mary, Servant of the Lord .......................................... 41
The Innkeeper ............................................................. 45
Temple Dwellers .......................................................... 49
The Visit of the Wise Men ......................................... 53
Grieving Mothers' Day in Court ................................ 59
The Judge Instructs the Jury ...................................... 69
The Verdict is In ......................................................... 73
The Grand Finale ....................................................... 81

Conclusion ................................................................... 83

*Dedication*

To my two brothers, five sisters,
two children, and grandchildren

for your love, understanding,
fellowship, and encouragement.

You are among some of the greatest gifts
God has bestowed upon me.

# ALSO BY CLAUDETTE FRANCIS

## THE MYSTERY OF THE RESURRECTION
An Inspirational Drama on the Resurrection of Jesus Christ . . . with Testimonies from high-profile star witnesses

## JESUS IS RISEN
An Easter Play for Children

## CHILDREN'S BIBLE STORIES WORKBOOK
Stories from the New Testament
(Child's Book)

## CHILDREN'S BIBLE STORIES WORKBOOK
Stories from the New Testament
(Teacher's Edition with Answers)

# NOTE ABOUT THIS BOOK
## (Disclaimer)

The information in this book is a combination of fact and fiction. The author used imagination and the Biblical story of the events surrounding the birth of Jesus, to create this Spiritual fiction. No responsibility is therefore assumed for any problems arising from decisions taken by readers, based on their interpretation of issues and events contained in this book.

Neither is there any responsibility assumed for any problem arising from decisions taken by readers based on their interpretation of the judicial process as contained in this book.

Claudette Francis
Toronto, Ontario, Canada

# FOREWORD

I am honored to write this foreword for "THE MYSTERY OF THE NATIVITY OF JESUS". There are two sections under which I will make my references.

In the first section, Claudette Francis' inspirational drama "THE MYSTERY OF THE NATIVITY OF JESUS" is commendable. She has shown her ability to intertwine the spiritual with the everyday occurrences and the tumultuous happenings of our daily lives. It was in her early childhood days that Claudette first began to conceptualize short plays for the catechetical summer school program in Guyana. From then onwards all her studies and her sensitive spiritual insight became her absorbing interest. She has perfected many collections such as "THE MYSTERY OF THE RESURRECTION" which is her inspirational drama on the RESURRECTION OF JESUS CHRIST. I am sure that the fruits of her long and sanctified labors presented here in "THE MYSTERY OF THE NATIVITY OF JESUS" will serve to stretch, strengthen and deepen our faith in Jesus, the Son of God.

Secondly, I have read with great interest Claudette Francis' inspirational drama on the "MYSTERY OF THE NATIVITY OF JESUS". It is beautifully done. The use of her imagination and the Biblical stories of the events surrounding the birth of Jesus are extraordinary. Francis really captured the drama of the environment during the time of the Nativity of Jesus. Claudette is a playwright with extraordinary gifts at visualizing the scenery and transforming it into real visual occurrences based upon the Gospel readings. She does so in a very coherent and truly convincing manner. Into this inspirational drama the "MYSTERY OF THE NATIVITY OF JESUS", the author has put a life's experience of growing up with Christ. Her book is a wonderful story of faith. It is a highly spiritual drama that brings vivid pictures of the events to my mind. I would encourage everyone to read it.

Bernadette Nelberta Swan, BA, M.T.S.
Founder: Bernadette N. Swan Social Care Foundation
Canada, Alberta, Edmonton
September, 2012

# AUTHOR'S ACKNOWLEDGEMENTS

The author gratefully acknowledges the work of her parents who first exposed her to the ideals of the Christian faith, and planted the Word of God in her heart. In addition, she acknowledges the support of the vibrant Christian community at the Annunciation Church, Malgré Tout, West Bank Demerara, Guyana, South America.

To all her students, well-wishers, and participants, both in Guyana and Canada, who encouraged her to develop this fictional, dramatic version of the Mystery of the Nativity of Jesus, a heartfelt thanks to you.

Lastly, she expresses her deep appreciation to Fran Richardson, Diploma in Lay Ministry, and Enid Ferdinand, BA—Proof Reader/Editorial Services, for their various contributions, providing careful reading, good advice, and valuable recommendations.

To God be the glory, honor, praise, and thanksgiving!

**GLAD TIDINGS**

# INTRODUCTION

THE MYSTERY OF THE NATIVITY is the third in a series of spiritual fiction written for entertainment, enjoyment and inspiration. 'The Mystery of the Resurrection' and 'Jesus is Risen,' have already received great commendation from many readers.

Acting out Biblical stories played a vital part in my own religious formation. In researching and writing this drama, I was reminded of my involvement in the Christmas Plays in my school concerts at the end of the year. As if not to be outdone, our parish church was also the venue for Christmas pageants. It was not unusual for my parents to wake up their children at 10:p.m. on Christmas Eve Night, help them get dressed in their costumes as shepherds or angels, as the case might be, then walk them to the parish church to join with other children in participating in the joyful Midnight Christmas Service.

Working with these Biblical stories, gave me a vital understanding of Jesus as he is. I accept him as my role model, and put into practice the wisdom he taught his followers.

The Mystery of the Nativity of Jesus is a delightful book. The facts and events are taken from the Bible, and the drama is written in a contemporary format. My hope

*Claudette Francis*

is that everyone who reads this book will be inspired to do some Bible research on their own and demonstrate their own spiritual connections to Jesus even more deeply.

Note: Some fictional names have been given to many of the characters in this drama. I hope that this will make for more interesting reading.

Claudette Francis
4-170 Brickworks Lane
Toronto, Ontario, Canada
M6N 5H7

# CAST OF CHARACTERS

- Judge Deborah
- Bailiff
- Madam G. Louisburg, the Prosecutor
- King Herod
- Angel Gabriel
- Shepherds
- Joseph
- Mary
- The Innkeeper
- Simeon and Anna
- Wise Men
- Rachel and Companions
- Spectators
- The Forewoman of the Jury
- Marshal
- The Press
- Jesus

# Scene 1

## King Herod Defends Himself

*Enter King Herod the Great*

Judge: [To the Prosecutor] Madam Louisburg, what is the charge?

Prosecutor: Your Honor, the charges against King Herod are multiple. He is charged with the following counts:

1. Lies and deception
2. Denying the birth of Jesus, the Messiah, and King of the Jews
3. Attempted murder of the said Jesus, the Messiah, King of the Jews
4. Crimes against humanity. King Herod ordered the massacre of all the boys in and around Bethlehem who were two years old or under.

Judge: Thank you, Madam Louisburg, the charges have been laid.

Prosecutor: Your Honor, King Herod the Great will be conducting his own defense.

Judge: [to King Herod] State your name and address.

King Herod: [full of confidence] Your Honor, my name is King Herod the Great, but sometimes I am also called King Herod 1, or King Herod the First.

Judge: Very well King Herod the Great, King Herod 1, or King Herod the First, in this courtroom you will be called King Herod.

Period. Madam Louisburg this court awaits your opening remarks.

Prosecutor: Your Honor. The Crown alleges that at the time of the nativity of Jesus, the Messiah, and King of the Jews, King Herod was the ruling monarch. Even though the Messiah was born in King Herod's jurisdiction, he knew nothing about it until some wise men from the East came to Jerusalem and asked him, "Where is the child who has been born king of the Jews?

For we observed his star at its rising, and have come to pay him homage?" (Matthew 2:2) Since he was unable to answer the question, King Herod called together all the chief priests and scribes of the people and enquired of them where the Messiah was to be born. They told him in Bethlehem of Judea. (Matthew 2: 1-5) Herod then related this information to the wise men and told them to go and search diligently for the child and when they had found him they were to bring him word so that he may also go and pay him homage. (Matthew 2: 8-9) It turned out that the wise men did not return to Herod. When Herod realized that he had been tricked by the wise men, he was infuriated, and he sent and killed all the boys in and around Bethlehem who were two years old or under, according to the time that he had learned from the wise men. (Matthew 2: 16)

King Herod: I categorically deny all the charges leveled against me, and confess that I did nothing wrong. This is nothing more but a vicious conspiracy to frame me for these atrocities.

Judge: Have no fear, King Herod. It will be up to a jury to prove your innocence or guilt. They will decide whether you did anything wrong or right. King Herod what is your address?

King Herod: Your Honor, my address is the King's Own Palace, Jerusalem.

Judge: The charges against you are multiple.

Count 1. Lies and deception

Count 2. Denying the birth of Jesus, the Messiah, and king of the Jews.

Count 3. Attempted murder of the said Jesus, the Messiah, and king of the Jews.

Count 4. Crimes against humanity. King Herod you ordered the massacre of all the boys in and around Bethlehem who were two years old or under.

How do you plead, King Herod?

King Herod: [in a clear voice] Not guilty, Your Honor.

Judge: What do you know about the king of the Jews?

King Herod: King of the Jews? Not so, Your Honor, no king of the Jews was born in my Kingdom. That is mere fantasy! I am the king of the Jews! Your Honor, the problem with this mistaken identity of the king of the Jews, is that it spreads confusion throughout my Kingdom. Your Honor, there is a conspiracy to frame me and make me look evil in the sight of my people.

Judge: King Herod, let me remind you that this matter is now in the hands of a judiciary, and consequently, it is up to this court to determine what is fantasy, conspiracy and fallacy. What else do you know about the wise men from the East and the king of the Jews?

Your Honor, I was alone at home in my palace, one day, when I heard a tumult outside the walls of the palace. I called the chief priests and scribes and demanded they investigate the origin of that tumult.

Judge: Tell this court what that tumult was all about.

King Herod: Your Honor, it turned out that some so-called wise men from the East came to town that night, and they asked, "Where is the child that has been born the king of the Jews, for we observed his star at the rising and have come to pay him homage?" (Matthew 2: 1-2)

Judge: King Herod, I submit to you that the new king of the Jews was your rival, and so it was your intention to do away with him.

King Herod: No, Your Honor, my intentions were honorable.

Judge: Were you not the king at that time?

King Herod: Yes, certainly Your Honor. I was indeed the reigning monarch at the time.

Judge: Was there not a protocol of succession to the throne?

King Herod: Yes, certainly Your Honor.

Judge: Wasn't it a known fact that one of your sons or daughters would succeed you on the throne?

King Herod: Yes, certainly that was the case, Your Honor.

Judge: King Herod, did any of your subjects referred to you as a weakling?

Prosecutor: [interrupting] Your Honor, I beg to question the relevance of such frivolous and tedious questioning of the defendant.

Judge: Should I not try to elicit from the defendant a reason for his irrational fear, Madam Louisburg? Allow this judicial inquiry to continue, and let the accused speak for himself.

King Herod: Your Honor, for the record I would say, "I am not a weakling, but I would admit I was frightened, I was puzzled, I was perplexed, and I was irritated at being faced with such an imminent dilemma. Yes, I might have acted irrationally, but believe me, I did nothing wrong."

Prosecutor: Your Honor, King Herod, acted by ordering the massacre of infants, innocent little baby boys who did him no harm. His reaction was indeed very irrational. He said so himself. He actually declared war on innocent babes and their parents.

Judge: Thank you, Madam Louisburg. Let the accused defend his actions. What happened next, King Herod?

King Herod: Your Honor I wanted to go and worship that baby, but the wise men tricked me.

In other words, they stood me up, Your Honor!

Prosecutor: That is indeed the kind of deception of which King Herod is capable. He had no intention of going to worship the king of the Jews, and he knows it, Your Honor.

Judge: Did you ever see the wise men again?

King Herod: No, Your Honor, and that was the end of that! You see, Your Honor, I waited, and waited, and waited on those guys to return, but they never did return to me. They deceived me, Your Honor.

Judge: Are you insinuating that the wise men disappeared mysteriously?

King Herod: Yes, Your Honor, that's it! I refer to this whole escapade as, 'The Mystery of the Lost Wise Men.' If you want my candid opinion of this whole affair I would state categorically that these guys were spies from the East coming to spy out my land, and overthrow my government.

Prosecutor: Your Honor, King Herod acted on the spur of the moment, became disillusioned, and did what was wrong in the sight of his people. It is inconceivable that a man of his stature should do such a thing. He grossly misunderstood the role of the wise men. There is not one shred of evidence to prove that the wise men were spies. Their mission was merely to search for a child.

Judge: [abruptly] King Herod, you may go.

[To the Bailiff] Call the next witness.

*Exit King Herod*

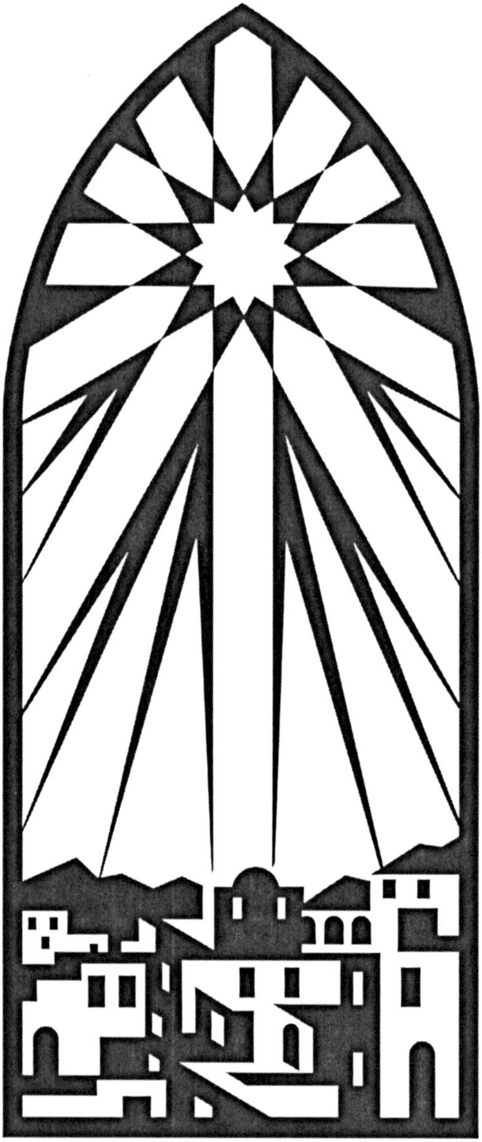

# Scene 2

# Angels Announce Jesus' Birth

Enter 12 men and women in angels' costumes.

Judge: Only one of you will testify on behalf of all of your fellow angels.

*[Angel Gabriel steps forward.]*

Angel Gabriel: [excited] I am the one, Your Honor. I will speak on behalf of the angels.

Judge: State your full name and address.

Angel Gabriel: My name is Angel Gabriel, I live in the Spiritual Realm, Seventh Heaven, High Court 1 A.

Judge: What do you know about the Nativity of Jesus?

Angel Gabriel: Your Honor, I happen to know everything.

Judge: Tell this court what you know.

Angel Gabriel: [confidently] Your Honor, from the beginning, the first woman, Eve and the first man, Adam missed the mark that the Lord God had set up for them. They fell for Satan's deception and preferred to listen to him rather than the Lord God. They disobeyed the Lord God's instructions and committed a sin. However, in His mercy, even though the Lord God condemned them for their sin, He also made them a promise. He promised to send them a Messiah from heaven to redeem, not only them, but all who would come after them.

Judge: [puzzled] Explain what you meant by the term, 'missed the mark.'

Angel Gabriel: Your Honor, there is a simple word for 'missed the mark'; it is 'sinned,' but mortals rarely use that word today. They prefer to be politically correct, and instead of using the word 'sinned,' they use 'missed the mark.' Yes, that is more politically correct, so they say; it does not offend anyone, you see. To use the word 'sinned' shows insensitivity.

Judge: [in awe] Thank you, Angel Gabriel, for the lesson on political correctness. Now, continue with your testimony.

Angel Gabriel: Yes, Your Honor. I will.

Judge: [leaning back in her seat] This court is listening.

Angel Gabriel: So in the fullness of time, God kept His promise. He sent me to a town in Galilee, called Nazareth, to a virgin engaged to a man whose name was Joseph of the

*The Mystery of the Nativity*

house of David. The virgin's name was Mary. (Luke 1: 26-27) I brought the message from the LORD GOD to Mary.

Judge: What was the content of your message?

Angel Gabriel: Your Honor, pardon my boldness, but I am sorry, I cannot divulge that kind of information. It is top secret! I would certainly be breaching heavenly security by divulging such information. I crave your indulgence on this matter.

Judge: [puzzled] Was the defendant, King Herod, informed of any of the heavenly plan?

Angel Gabriel: No, Your Honor, but even if he had heard the message, he would not have believed any of it. In King Herod's mind, the whole Mystery of the Nativity of Jesus is a hoax and a joke. Suffice it to say, he acted imprudently when he heard that a King of the Jews had been born in his Kingdom.

Judge: Explain what you mean by this statement.

Angel Gabriel: Obviously, his actions were driven by his goal-orientated mindset. He wanted to consolidate his dynasty, he wanted to be the King of the Jews, he wanted to protect his family line, and he wanted to beef up his image among his people; therefore he could not tolerate the idea of a rival king in his Kingdom. Ultimately, he thought of a malicious plan to get rid of this rival king.

The trouble is he obviously went too far in trying to achieve his goal.

Judge: [abruptly] Angel Gabriel, you may go, and take the other angels with you.

Bailiff, call the next witness.

*Exit the angels*

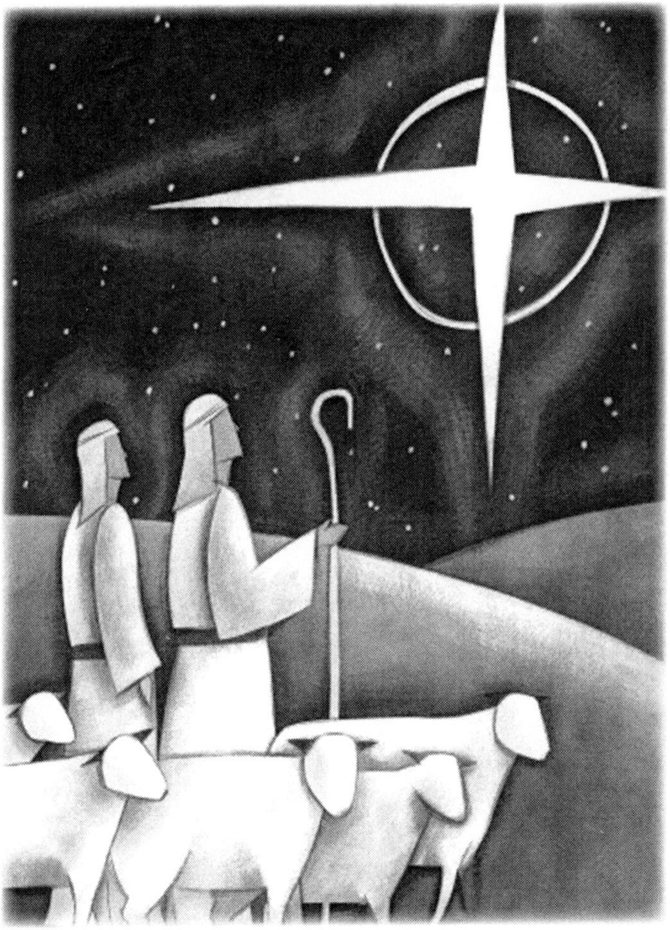

# Scene 3

# Shepherds Receive the Good News

*Enter 12 shepherds, men and women]*

Judge: Only one of you will testify on behalf of all of your fellow shepherds.

*[One shepherd steps forward.]*

Judge: State your full name and address.

Shepherd: Your Honor, my name is Shepherd Ess, Number 1112. I live in the fields of Bethlehem, on the North side.

Judge: What do you know about the Nativity of Jesus?

Shepherd Ess: Your Honor, we were all keeping watch over our flocks by night when an angel of the Lord stood before us, and the glory of the Lord shone around us, and we were terrified. (Luke 2: 8-9)

Judge: What did the angel of the Lord say to you?

Shepherd Ess: Your Honor, the angel said, "Do not be afraid; for see, I am bringing you news of great joy for all the people." (Luke 2:10)

Judge: [rubbing her hands together] What was the good news?

Shepherd Ess: Your Honor, the angel of the Lord continued, "to you is born this day in the city of David a Savior, who is the Messiah, the Lord." (Luke 2:11)

Judge: Is that the full message?

Shepherd Ess: No, Your Honor. The angel also said, "This will be a sign to you, you will find the infant wrapped in bands of cloth and lying in a manger." (Luke 2:12)

Judge: What followed after the angel of the Lord gave his message? Did you decide to investigate?

Shepherd Ess: Yes, Your Honor, but suddenly there was with the angel a multitude of the heavenly host, praising God and saying, "Glory to God in the highest heaven, and on earth peace among those whom He favors." (Luke 2: 13-14)

Judge: continue. This is truly a story for the Press.

Shepherd Ess: Certainly, Your Honor, the Press would have been delighted to get hold of a story such as this, but for our part when the angels had left us and gone back to heaven, we said to one another . . . [All begin speaking together] "Let us go over to Bethlehem and see this thing that has taken place which the Lord . . .

*The Mystery of the Nativity*

Judge: [interrupting] Order in this court!

We must have order! Order!! She strikes her gavel once. You were told that only one person will testify on behalf of all of you.

This is a court of law, not the market place.

Let us continue with the evidence in an atmosphere of utmost decorum.

Shepherd Ess: Yes, Your Honor. We all decided to set out and see this thing that had taken place, which the Lord had made known to us. (Luke 2: 15)

Prosecutor: What a marvelous idea, Your Honor! To think that the Lord God would communicate His plans in such a spectacular fashion to lowly shepherds—poor, uneducated, lowly men and women, is absolutely beyond my wildest imagination.

Judge: Thank you Madam Louisburg. We would rather listen to the witness, if you do not mind. Continue Shepherd Ess.

Shepherd Ess: Your Honor, we went with haste and found Mary and Joseph and the child lying in the manger. When we saw this, we made known what had been told about the child, and all who heard it were amazed at what we had told them. (Luke 2:16-18)

Judge: What were your feelings as you proclaimed the news?

Shepherd Ess: We were overjoyed to be treated like Royals. Can you imagine what it was like to have angels from the Royal throne in heaven, bring us a message from the King of Heaven?

Judge: [startled] So what was your response to such overwhelming news?

Shepherd Ess: Your Honor, we simply returned glorifying and praising God for all we had heard and seen. (Luke 2:20) That is our story and we stand by every word of it.

That is the Mystery of the Nativity. God kept His promise and we were the first to see the fulfillment of the promise.

Judge: Now Shepherd Ess, what do you know about King Herod? He stands accused of lies, deception, attempted murder, and the massacre of infant boys.

Shepherd Ess: [rolling eyes] Seriously, Your Honor, we beg to inform you that we know nothing about the accused King Herod. We are not implicated in the doings of the King. To him, we are deemed to be people on the periphery, outcasts, marginalized, and uneducated.

Prosecutor: Indeed Your Honor, that is precisely how these hard working citizens were looked upon by the defendant, King Herod.

Judge: Continue Shepherd Ess.

Shepherd Ess: Your Honor, King Herod is a very strange fellow who passes strange edicts into law. We keep our distance. Our minds are on our sheep. We certainly take care of our own business. We have never gone to the palace, and we certainly do not intend to go there, not now, nor in the future.

Judge: [exasperated] You may go Shepherd Ess, and take all of the other shepherds with you. [To the Bailiff] Call the next witness.

*Exit the shepherds*

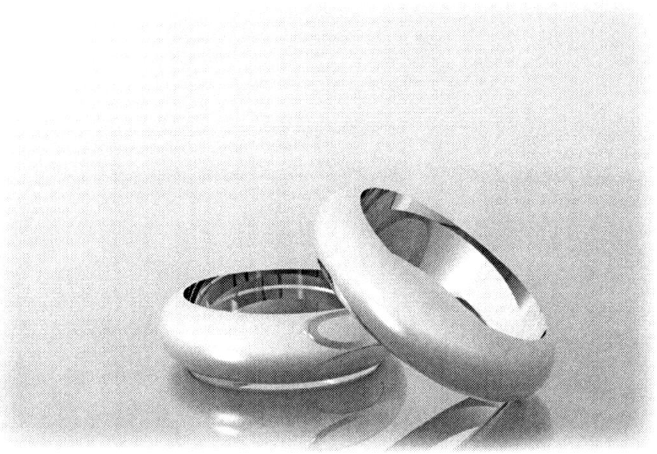

# Scene 4

# Joseph, A Man of Integrity

*Enter Joseph*

Judge: State your name and address.

Joseph: Your Honor, I am Joseph and I live in Nazareth

Prosecutor: Your Honor, here is a witness who knows exactly what took place. I would advise you to question him thoroughly, but I must also warn you that his testimony may contain graphic details of what really happened to him.

Judge: *[Quite taken back by this remark]* Thank you Madam Louisburg for your very candid assessment of the character of this witness. Joseph, to the best of your recollection, what do you know about the events surrounding the nativity of Jesus?

Joseph: Your Honor, I have to be honest with you. I am a humble man, a righteous man, a noble man, a man of integrity, and honor.

Judge: Joseph, your credentials are very impressive, but let us get on with the trial.

Joseph: The story begins like this. I was engaged to be married to my fiancée, Mary, but before we lived together, she was found to be with child from the Holy Spirit. (Matthew 1:18)

Judge: How did you handle that predicament?

Joseph: *[looking puzzled]* Your Honor, I was very puzzled, to say the least, but because I am a man of integrity I did not really want to bring my fiancée to public shame, so I considered putting her away secretly.

Judge: Did you do it?

Joseph: No, Your Honor. Just then an angel of the LORD appeared to me in a dream and said, "Joseph, son of David . . ."

Judge: Angels, Angels, Angels! How astonishing! What sort of busy bodies are these angels? Were you ever in the company of an angel before?

Joseph: Your Honor, the answer to your first question is: "Angels are not busy bodies, they are busy spirits."

The answer to your second question is:
"No, I was never in the company of an angel before."

Judge: Very well, Joseph, what else did the angel tell you?

Joseph: Your Honor, the angel continued, "Do not be afraid to take Mary as your wife, for the child conceived in her is from the Holy Spirit. She will bear a Son and you are to name him Jesus. He will save his people from their sins." (Matthew 1:20-21)

Judge: *[quite pleased]* This is very interesting stuff, Joseph. Please continue.

Joseph: You see, Your Honor, the birth of Jesus was prophesied thousands of years before it actually happened.

Some of the prophets reached out into the future and saw this thing which would eventually come to pass and they kept telling the people that it was coming. Also, God Himself had promised a Messiah. Now the time had come for Him to fulfill His promise.

Judge: How do you know that? How do you know that God was ready to fulfill His promise.

Joseph: [full of confidence] Your Honor, My God does not lie. My God keeps His word, and when He says something will happen, it will surely come to pass.

Judge: Thank you, Joseph. Now to the more serious question. What do you know about the defendant, King Herod?

Joseph: Your Honor, King Herod is in a class by himself.

Judge: [puzzled] Explain your assertion.

Prosecutor: Your Honor, if I may interject here, Joseph means that King Herod is not like you and me. He did some very atrocious things which made him different from every other person.

No other person would have thought of doing the things that this defendant, King Herod did.

Judge: Thank you for your input, Madam Louisburg.

Joseph: Your Honor, King Herod heard about the birth of the child Jesus and he was very frightened, because he felt that the child was a direct threat to him and his kingdom. Yes, Jesus had become his competition, his rival, so to speak. So he put out an edict which in effect called for the shedding of innocent blood.

Judge: Are you insinuating that he tried to kill the Child Jesus?

Joseph: Yes, Your Honor that is precisely what I am saying. King Herod planned to eliminate the child, so there would be no insurrection in the Kingdom, but, an angel of the LORD appeared to me . . .

Judge: [interrupting] in a dream . . .

Joseph: Yes, Your Honor. How did you know that?

Judge: [ignoring the question] Carry on with your testimony, Joseph.

Joseph: You see, Your Honor, angels are messengers from God. They visit the earthly realm to bring messages from the heavenly Kingdom.

Judge: What did the angel say this time?

Joseph: Your Honor he said, "Get up, take the child and his mother and flee to Egypt and remain there until I tell you, for Herod is about to search for the child to destroy him." (Matthew 2:13) So I got up immediately, woke Mary and the baby, and under cover of darkness, saddled the donkey and we took off for Egypt.

Judge: Joseph, let us get back to your testimony of King Herod, the accused.

Joseph: Your Honor, King Herod is a very insecure man. He rules with an iron fist. He is a ruthless dictator who lacks confidence. He is emotionally unstable, to say the least.

Judge: Joseph, you may go.

Bailiff, call the next witness.

*Exit Joseph*

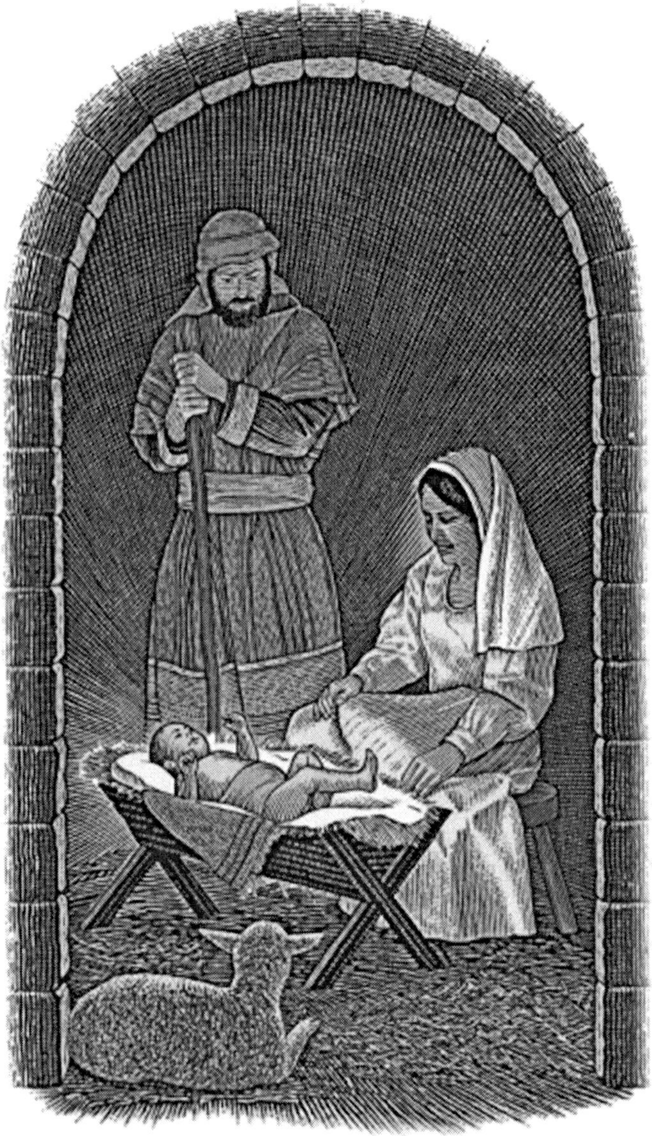

# Scene 5

# Mary, Servant of the Lord

*Enter Mary*

Judge: Mary, what do you know about the events surrounding the nativity of Jesus?

Mary: [with boldness] Your Honor, God's people had grown tired of the tyranny and injustices which were being meted out to them by the foreign occupiers of their land. Consequently, they were looking forward to a better life for themselves and their families. They knew that the only one who could relieve them from the burden of pain and frustration was the Messiah, Jesus. God heard the prayers of His people and decided to fulfill His promise to them. I was chosen to be the mother of the Messiah Jesus, and when the fullness of time had come, God sent His angel Gabriel to announce the great news to me.

Judge: What did the angel actually say to you?

Mary: Your Honor the Angel Gabriel said, "Greetings, favored one. The Lord is with you!" (Luke 1:28)

Judge: How did you respond to such an angelic greeting?

Mary: Your Honor, I was very perplexed by his words and pondered what sort of greeting this might be. (Luke 1:29) Then the angel spoke again.

Judge: And what did he say this time?

Mary: He said, "Do not be afraid, Mary, for you have found favour with God. And now you will conceive in your womb and bear a Son and you will name him Jesus. He will be great and he shall be called the Son of the Most High, and the Lord God will give him the throne of his ancestor, David. He will reign over the house of Jacob forever, and of his kingdom there will be no end." (Luke 1:30-33)

Judge: Did you think of asking the angel how this would be accomplished?

Mary: Yes, of course Your Honor, I did. I asked, "How can this be since I am a virgin?" (Luke 1:34)

Judge: And what was the heavenly reply?

Mary: Your Honor, Gabriel said, "The Holy Spirit will come upon you, and the power of the Most High will overshadow you; therefore the child to be born will be holy, he will be called the Son of God." (Luke 1:35)

Judge: Is that the whole story, Mary?

Mary: No, Your Honor. The angel had more to say. He said, "And now, your relative Elizabeth in her old age has also conceived a son; and this is the sixth month for her who was called barren. For nothing shall be impossible with God." (Luke 1:36-37)

Judge: Is that the end of your testimony?

Mary: Your Honor, forgive me for speaking again. Before the angel departed I gave my full consent to God. I said, "Here I am, the servant of the Lord, let it be done with me according to Your Word." (Luke 1: 38)

Then the angel departed.

Judge: What was God's purpose for sending His Son to earth?

Mary: Your Honor that is what the Mystery of the Nativity of Jesus is all about. Jesus was sent to redeem humanity from sin. He did not come to condemn humanity, but through his suffering, death, burial, and resurrection humanity would be saved. This is good news, Your Honor.

Judge: Tell this court what you know about the accused, King Herod.

Mary: Shortly after my baby was born my family and I had to flee to a foreign land, because the King was seeking to destroy my baby boy.

Judge: In your estimation, what kind of man is he?

Mary: He is very proud, selfish, and ruthless.

Prosecutor: Your Honor, if I may interject here, I would say that King Herod's behavior is reprehensible. He assuredly portrayed a dual personality. He acted with prejudice and malice aforethought in ordering the massacre of countless baby boys, so as to make sure that he was not dethroned.

Judge: Madam Louisburg, allow this trial to run its course, and the court will make its decision. You may go, Mary.

*Exit Mary*

Judge: Bailiff, this trial is adjourned. I will see everyone back in court tomorrow at 9 a.m. standard time.

Bailiff: This Court is adjourned. The judge will see everyone back in court tomorrow at 9 a.m. standard time. All rise!

*Exit Judge Deborah.*
*Everyone else follows.*

# Scene 6

# The Innkeeper

*Enter the Innkeeper*

Judge: State your name and address.

Innkeeper: My name is simply Mr. Innkeeper

And my address is Bethlehem, on the North side.

Judge: What can you tell this court about the events surrounding the Nativity of Jesus?

Mr. Innkeeper: Emperor Augustus sent out a decree that the entire world should be registered. (Luke 2:1*)* This compelled the people to return to their ancestral homes and be counted, you know, something like taking a census.

Judge: Was this decree good or bad for the economy?

Mr. Innkeeper: Your Honor, it was really good news for the economy and in particular for me. I was considering filing for bankruptcy, but the emperor's decree changed my plans. I knew that as a businessman, my business would flourish. I knew for a fact that my inn was going to be filled to capacity all during the census taking, and so it happened. Myriads of travelers descended upon the town, and before long my inn was full.

Judge: Then what did you do? Did you have the time to build bigger inns?

Mr. Innkeeper: No, Your Honor. I had enough reservations to deal with. At last two travelers, a man and his pregnant wife appeared and knocked on my door wanting to get in for the night. But my inn was already full. And there was a sign on the door which read, "NO VACANCIES."

When these lowly travelers approached me, I told them there was no place for them in the inn. *(Luke 2:7)*

Judge: So what became of the man and his pregnant wife?

Mr. Innkeeper: It is true I had no place in my inn, but I had a stable and I sent them there.

The next thing I heard was that a special new-born King was born in my stable.

Judge: Thank you Mr. Innkeeper. Now let us turn to the case in question. What can you tell this court about the accused King Herod?

Mr. Innkeeper: Not very much, Your Honor. We, the innkeepers never discuss the King. We are not acquaintances. As for me personally, I am a poor innkeeper and he is a rich, powerful King. We do not mingle together, but I heard, through the grapevine, that he ordered his soldiers to kill all of the baby boys in Bethlehem and its vicinity in the hope of killing that special King that was born in my stable.

Judge: Why did he go to such lengths?

Mr. Innkeeper: Your Honor, King Herod is the kind of guy who would not let anything or anyone get in the way of his own will. As far as I am concerned, he is a tyrant, a dictator, and a crazy guy.

Prosecutor: [interrupting] And he was a murderer too, do not forget that.

Judge: Thank you Mr. Innkeeper. Please remember that the accused is innocent until proven guilty by a court of law, and besides, this court is no place for hearsay or gossip.

You may go, Mr. Innkeeper. Bailiff, call the next witness.

*Exit Mr. Innkeeper*

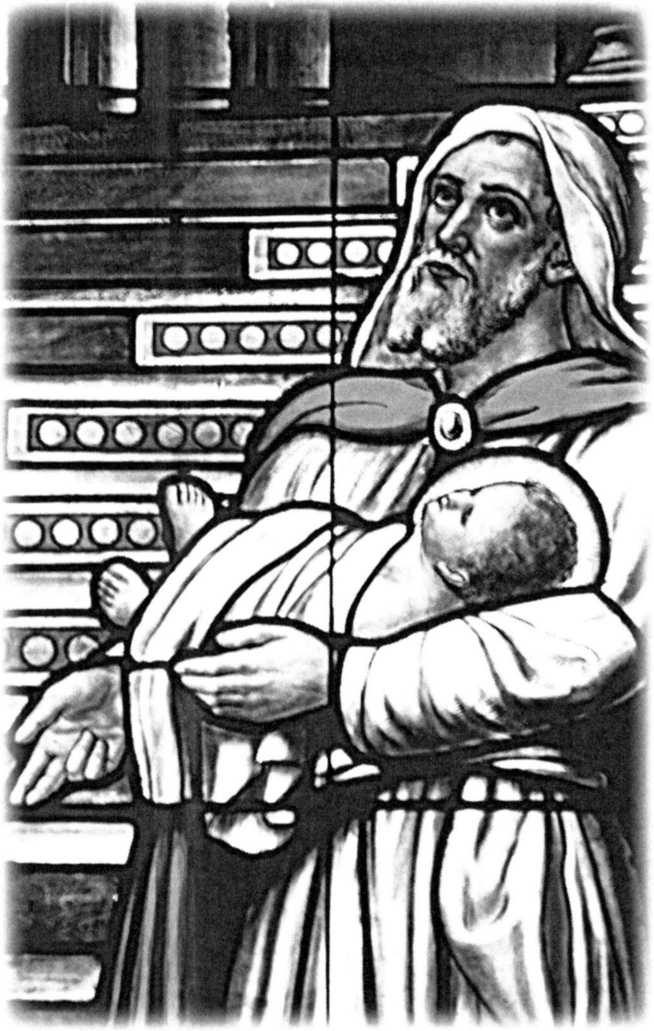

# Scene 7

## Temple Dwellers

*Enter Simeon and Anna*

Judge: Simeon *[Simeon steps forward] State your full address.*

Simeon: Your Honor, I live in the Temple at Jerusalem, and day after day I was waiting for the fulfillment of a promise that was made to me.

Judge: Explain yourself, Simeon.

Simeon: The Holy Spirit had given me a revelation. He revealed to me that I would not see death before I had seen the Lord's Messiah.

Judge: What is your profession?

Simeon: I am a prophet. I see parents bringing their children into the temple to offer them up to the Lord.

Prosecutor: Simeon, answer only the question put to you. Do not volunteer any further details. It constitutes uncalled for detraction from the case.

*Claudette Francis*

Judge: Shall we continue Madam Louisburg? For how long were you at this post, Simeon?

Simeon: For as long as I can remember.

Judge: So that means you must have seen thousands of parents bringing their children to the temple, is that so?

Simeon: Yes, Your Honor, by the thousands they come, year after year.

Judge: What made you think that this particular child was different from all the other children brought to the temple?

Simeon: Your Honor, God revealed the nature of the child to me, long before he was born. Then the Holy Spirit led me into the temple at the very moment that his parents brought in the child to be presented to the Lord. I blessed him and I said to his Mother Mary, "This child is destined for the falling and the rising of many in Israel, and to be a sign that will be opposed so that the inner thoughts of many will be revealed and a sword will pierce your own soul." (Luke 2:43-35)

Judge: Now Simeon, to the business at hand. What do you know about the accused, King Herod?

Simeon: Your Honor, I know very little about the King. You can ask the prophetess, Anna. She is in a better position to fill you in on the goings-on in the kingdom. She has lived in the temple, for as far back as I can remember. She witnesses parents bringing their babies into the temple on a regular basis, and she gets caught up with the local news.

*The Mystery of the Nativity*

Judge: Oh, she does, does she? Very well Simeon, you may step aside.

Prosecutor: Your Honor, these two witnesses, Simeon and Anna, are devoted servants of the Living God. They know full well what His promises were, and they waited patiently for the fulfillment of those promises. They are telling the truth, the whole truth, and nothing but the truth.

Judge: Thank you Madam Louisburg, the court will decide who is telling the truth, the whole truth, and nothing but the truth.

*[Simeon takes a few steps backwards, and Anna moves to the front. The judge now questions Anna.]*

Judge: Explain your role in the temple.

Anna: Your Honor, I never leave the temple. I worship there with fasting and praying day and night. Your Honor, when I beheld the child, I knew exactly who he was, and I began to praise God and to speak about the child to all who were looking for the redemption of Jerusalem. (Luke 2:36-38)

Judge: You have spoken very eloquently, Anna.

Thank you, and now, what do you know about the accused, King Herod?

Surely you must have heard about him.

Anna: Yes, Your Honor, I learned about him from the Scriptures. I studied the Scriptures through and through, and I knew that a king would try to kill this very child.

Judge: And did he do it?

Anna: No, Your Honor, but he tried. I heard the details from some of the mothers who brought their children to the temple.

He is ruthless, he is proud and he is merciless. This kind of behavior is not foreign to King Herod. This was the man who is known as a ruthless murderer. He executed several members of his own family including his wife and two sons.

Judge: [folding her hands on her lap]

Thank you, Prophetess Anna, you and Simeon may go.

Bailiff, call the next witness.

*Exit Simeon and Prophetess Anna*

# Scene 8

# The Visit of the Wise Men

*Enter about twenty-four persons dressed in eastern Kingly attire.*

Judge: Only one of you will testify on behalf of all of your fellow Wise Men.

*[Mecalph moves to the front]*

Prosecutor: Your Honor, please do not be harsh on the Wise Men. These are all we have coming out of the East. They are the happiest men on the face of the earth today. They are bringing good news about the Child Jesus.

Judge: The court will make that observation, Madam Louisburg [To Mecalph] For the record, state your full name and address.

Mecalph: Your Honor, my name is Mecalph, Wise Man # 0033. I am from the East in the Orient, and so is my entire entourage.

*[All of the wise men interject]*

Wise Men: So we are, Your Honor. We are the wise men from the East. Some people call us wise Men, some call us Magi, some call us astrologers, some call us magicians, and some call us sages. For our part, we answer to all the names thrown at us.

Judge: ORDER! ORDER!! *[Hits her gavel once]* Didn't we agree that only one of you will speak?

Wise Men: Yes, Your Honor, that is true; we apologize for our lapse of memory.

Judge: Very well, Mecalph you may continue. What was your mission here, in Jerusalem?

Mecalph: Your Honor we followed a star here. We came in search of a special child.

Judge: What special child? Do you mean the child known to all as the Messiah, the King of the Jews, and the Son of God?

You could not possibly mean that child . . . Could you?

Mecalph: Yes, Your Honor, without a doubt that was precisely the child for whom we searched. Your Honor we are a people who study the stars. That is our profession. We know what is going on in the universe, like we know the back of our hands. We perceive when something strange happens in the sky. We are the first to observe the phenomena, and we investigate.

Judge: Please be more specific.

*The Mystery of the Nativity*

Mecalph: Your Honor, we were exploring the skies when we saw an exceptionally bright star. Upon our investigation, we found out that that star meant that a new king was born in Bethlehem.

Judge: Did I miss something here. Are you implying that you have some kind of exceptional power to read the universe and interpret the stars?

Mecalph: Yes, Your Honor that is precisely what I mean.

Prosecutor: Your Honor, these wise men are exceptional. They have been endowed with what we call ESP, a sixth sense which sets them apart from the normal population.

Judge: Is this a fairy tale or what, Mecalph?

Mecalph: No, Your Honor. It was our duty to follow the star, and so we did. It took us roughly two years to get here, and our first stop was in Jerusalem.

Judge: Describe what happened when you arrived in Jerusalem.

Mecalph: Your Honor, we went to King Herod and enquired about the child. He had no idea what we were talking about.

Judge: So you are quite acquainted with the defendant, King Herod.

Prosecutor: Your Honor, King Herod made sure that everyone knew who he was. He had large sized images of himself plastered on walls, or set up in conspicuous places in the kingdom. He had monuments, buildings, grottoes, and well watered gardens built to honor him. He is by no means a shy man.

Judge: Thank you, Madam Louisburg for that auspicious profile of the King.

Judge: Mecalph, how well do you know the defendant?

Mecalph: Seriously, Your Honor, we cannot say we know him too well. All we know is that he learned from us the exact time when the star had appeared. Then he sent us to Bethlehem. He said, "Go and search diligently for the child and when you have found him, bring me word so that I may also go and pay him homage." (Matthew 2: 7-8)

Judge: Did you believe the King had any intentions of going to pay homage to the child king?

Mecalph: Yes, Your Honor, we actually believed him.

Judge: Would you say that he deceived you?

Mecalph: Certainly he did, and according to what we heard happened later, we have to agree that he did deceive us.

Judge: Did you find the Child?

Mecalph: Yes, Your Honor, we actually did find the Child. The star led us to the house where the Child was. We entered the house, we saw the Child with his mother, Mary, and we knelt down and paid him homage. Then opening our treasure chest, we offered him gold, frankincense and myrrh. (Matthew 2: 9-11)

Judge: [seemingly exhausted] Mecalph, is this the end of your testimony?

Mecalph: No, Your Honor, that night in a dream we were warned not to return to King Herod, and so we left for our country by another road. *(Matthew 2:12)*

Judge: Did it grieve you to learn that because of your failure to return to the king, he flew into a rage and ordered the massacre of countless innocent baby boys?

Mecalph: Certainly, Your Honor, we were very grieved to hear what had expired between the king and his subjects.

Obviously, he must have surmised that we were there to spy out his land, or overthrow his government, so in his angry rage he slew the boys.

Judge: Mecalph, you are dismissed. Take all the other wise men with you. [To the Bailiff] This court will be in recess for 60 minutes.

Bailiff: This court will be in recess for 60 minutes. All rise!

*Exit the judge and her court official. Everyone else follows.*

# Scene 9

# Grieving Mothers' Day in Court

*Enter a number of mothers*

Judge: Grieving mothers, the day has surely come for you to have your day in court.

Mothers: Thank you, Your Honor, we are certainly grateful to you. We are grieving the loss of our precious babies. A horrible act of injustice was perpetrated on us, and we cried until we had no more tears left in our eyes.

Judge: Relate to this court the circumstances surrounding your loss.

*[All of the mothers begin to give their testimonies at the same time.]*

ORDER! ORDER!! [the judge hits her gavel once] We will not have a riot in this court room. [*Many of the mothers sob openly. One mother is overcome with anguish and weeps loudly.*]

Spectators: [interrupt with loud whispers and groans ]

Judge: SILENCE in this court! No more interruption from you will be tolerated! [To the Bailiff] Remove the weeping mother from the court room.

*[The Bailiff rushes to obey the judge's instructions. He escorts the weeping mother out of the courtroom and into the waiting room. After the commotion subsides, Judge Deborah continues with the trial.]*

*[To the mothers] Let one person speak on your behalf.*

*[Luminca steps forward]*

Prosecutor: If I may speak, Your Honor, I would like to remind you that these are grieving mothers who need your compassion and the tolerance of this court. The mothers are here today seeking justice for their baby boys, who were denied justice for so long.

Judge: Must I remind everyone that this is a courtroom, and not a funeral home, nor a cemetery? Luminca, give us your testimony.

Luminca: Thank you, Your Honor; these are the facts as I recall them. On that most dreadful morning I was awakened by loud noises in the street. Looking through my window, I observed horses' hoofs pounding on the cobblestones, and soldiers shouting and pushing people around. I was appalled by the sight.

Judge: What did you think was going on?

Luminca: Your Honor, my first thoughts were that a parade of some sort was about to get underway, but as I looked more carefully, I observed His Majesty's soldiers fully dressed in royal regalia bouncing up and down on horses. Their spears were drawn, and they were shouting what sounded like profanity. The horses wore long cloaks over their backs, and they and their riders were running wild, in and out of houses, and in and out of courtyards. Your Honor, there was pandemonium in the street.

Judge: I can well imagine the chaos and confusion in the streets at that time. What else did you see, Luminca?

Luminca: I saw people running helter-skelter, some with babies in their arms, some with babies on their backs, and some with very young boys at their sides. They all seemed to be running away from some sort of dreaded monster. Worst of all, they looked to me as if they were in great pain.

Judge: What was your reaction?

Luminca: Your Honor, I was astonished to witness what was really happening. His Majesty's soldiers were driving their spears into the bodies of the babies and very young boys, and killing them right before their mothers' eyes.

Prosecutor: Your Honor, is that the way for a monarch to treat his citizens? His was the most gruesome act anyone has ever seen. It was a despicable act, to say the least.

Judge: We will get to the bottom of this, unbelievable incident, Madam Louisburg. Please, continue your testimony, Luminca.

Luminca: Your Honor, it was a dreadful sight. I turned away from the window to get my baby, but before I could escape through the back door, a soldier forced his way into my house and in a split second, he speared my son, and left him bleeding and lifeless in my arms.

*[Luminca falls to the floor shaking uncontrollably.]*

Spectators: [some begin sobbing, whispering and groaning]

Judge: For a second time I have to address my remarks to the spectators. Please, no more interruptions, or you will be escorted out of this courtroom, never to return!] [To the bailiff] Take Luminca out!

Prosecutor: Your Honor, the situation could only be described as complete mayhem in Bethlehem. Luminca is not over reacting, at all. King Herod perpetrated a murderous act devoid of humanitarian compassion and grace. Your Honor, Luminca described exactly what she witnessed the day she heard the blood of the Holy Innocents crying out to God from the ground. It was simply traumatic, to say the least!

Judge: [abruptly] *[to the Bailiff]* Court will be in recess and witnesses will resume their testimonies tomorrow at 10 a.m. standard time.

Bailiff: This court will be in recess until tomorrow at 10 a.m. standard time

All rise!

*Exit the judge and the court officials. Everyone else follows.*

## *[Court is once again in session.]*

Judge: Bailiff, call the next witness.

Bailiff: Roxanna!

Judge: Roxanna, can you corroborate Luminca's story?

Roxanna: Yes, Your Honor. I watched the whole ordeal from my basement window.

My initial reaction was that this was the end of the world. I had never before seen such chaos and confusion. Such a tragic event never happened in our town before. Your Honor, blood was everywhere!

Prosecutor: Your Honor, I would like to present exhibits numbers 1 to 4 of that tragic crime scene. *[Prosecutor produces four photographs depicting the cruelty and shame of King Herod's soldiers' despicable behavior.]* Your Honor, blood was squirting on the cobblestones like water running out of a pipe. The courtyards were soaked with blood. It was grotesque, to say the least.

Bodies of infants were strewn all over the place. It was truly a diabolic act.

Judge: [to the Bailiff] Submit the photographs as evidence] *[the bailiff walks over to the prosecutor, takes the photographs and hands them to the judge who carefully surveys them before continuing with the trial]*

We will get to the bottom of this barbaric event. What, in your opinion, was the reason for all this carnage?

Roxanna: Your Honor, an evil king was trying to defend his throne, but his actions caused untold grief to countless mothers.

They threw themselves beside their dying, and dead boys, as they wailed and wept profusely. They refused to be comforted, because their boys were no more.

Rachel was one of them. She knows what it is to have no comfort.

She knows what it is to lose her boys to the king's butchers.

Judge: So both you and Rachel witnessed those young boys going to their horrible, untimely deaths!

Roxanna: Yes, Your Honor, I would never want to relive that terrible time. I still have nightmares on account of what I witnessed on that dreadful day.

Judge: *[calling on Rachel]* Rachel, what is your testimony?

Rachel: *[distraught, and shaking]* It all happened because we had a mentally deranged King on the throne. But not only that, I think that the birth of Jesus the Messiah was truly behind all the carnage.

The whole idea of a genocide originated in the mind of a desperate King Herod, who could not see himself giving up his throne to anyone, divine or human.

*The Mystery of the Nativity*

Judge: How desperate was he?

Rachel: Your Honor, King Herod could not imagine another king coming to unseat him, so he killed all the boys hoping that the newborn king will be killed as well.

Prosecutor: Your Honor, Rachel's testimony is vital to this case. Her testimony will help prove that King Herod was definitely upset over the news of a rival king, and planned his murderous rampage without one thought of these poor mothers who were about to lose their precious little boys.

Judge: Your advice is well taken, Madam Louisburg.

Prosecutor: Your Honor, these women have given you a true picture of the man who called himself King. He is the epitome of evil. He portrays the personality of a madman. Hopefully, this jury will prove me correct.

Judge: Very well, Madame Louisburg, we will wait for the court's verdict. Rachel you may go and take all the other mothers with you.

*Exit Rachel and the mothers*

[*The judge addresses King Herod*] King Herod, the witnesses have spoken, you have heard their testimonies, you may now proceed with your closing statement.

Herod: Your Honor, the witnesses have tried to bring my name down to the dust. I said in my opening statement, "I did nothing wrong." Now I repeat in my closing statement, "I did nothing wrong." My throne was threatened by some imposters posing as wise men from the East. I had to act, quickly, Your Honor. To the best of my knowledge I acted as prudently as I could. It was my right to defend my throne. Far be it from me to give up my throne to a non-existent baby Messiah, King of the Jews.

Your Honor, my life is at stake now, and my only hope is that these jurors will agree with me that I did nothing wrong. This concludes my closing statement, Your Honor.

Judge: Madam Louisburg, please proceed with your closing statement.

Prosecutor: Your Honor, we have heard the testimonies of a great number of witnesses.

They have portrayed King Herod, as a monster, evil, mentally deranged, devoid of compassion, only to mention a few of the expressions labeled on King Herod. That is certainly who he is. I say to you, Your Honor, the defendant's actions were utterly incomprehensible.

Can you imagine taking the lives of so many innocent baby boys, simply because a king was trying to find and kill his rival? Words cannot adequately express the feelings of the women who lost their precious boys to this butcher of Jerusalem. King Herod resorted to lies, deception, cruelty, anger and murder when the wise men did not return to him.

King Herod's sinister effort to kill the Child Jesus, is well documented. What further testimony do we need? There is no need for me to add even one iota to these allegations. Your Honor, the Crown rests its case.

Judge: *[to the bailiff]* This court will reconvene in 24 hours.

Bailiff: This court will reconvene in 24 hours. All rise!

*Exit Judge Deborah.
Everyone else follows.*

# Scene 10

# The Judge Instructs the Jury

*[Enter Judge Deborah]*

Judge : Ladies and Gentlemen of the Jury, you heard the evidence from several witnesses. Now, as jurors, this is your time to perform your duty to this nation. Because of the very serious nature of this case, this jury will be sequestered. How long the sequestration will last, is solely up to you. You can reach a verdict in hours, or days, or weeks or months. The outcome of this case is now in your hands. However, I must impress upon you the importance of reaching a verdict. Make every reasonable effort to do so. Consult with your fellow jurors, express your views and listen to one another. Before you leave for deliberations and reach your verdict, there are several items I have to bring to your attention:

1. To summarize, King Herod is charged with four counts of felony. He denies all wrong doing. He thinks that the charges were trumped up as some sort of conspiracy to dethrone him. However, his claim does nothing to appease these grieving mothers who lost so many of their children at the hands of king Herod's brutal soldiers. The grieving mothers

gave first hand experiences of the measure of their pain. As jurors, you must take into consideration all of the facts and evidence that you have seen and heard in this court.

2. King Herod's claim to having done nothing wrong does nothing to explain the heart-rending testimonies of so many witnesses, who declare that he was a downright liar, a deceiver, and a tyrant, that the killings were intentional in an effort to prevent Jesus from unseating him. Likewise, King Herod will no doubt argue that he was justified in protecting his crown, and he might have an argument there, so be it.

3. As jurors, it is your duty to weigh all of the facts and evidence in a calm and collected manner. Since the defendant pleaded not guilty, King Herod deserves a fair and unbiased trial. Likewise, the Crown deserves a resolution to this very grave matter.

4. The onus is now on you, six men and six women of this jury, to prove whether King Herod is guilty, as charged.

5. If your submission is that the defendant is guilty, then you must prove, beyond the shadow of a doubt, that he is guilty.

6. If during your discussions and deliberations, clarifications on any points are needed, please feel free to consult with me in chambers.

7. My final instruction to you is this: It is your duty to arrive at a just verdict after considering all of the facts and evidence presented during the course of this trial. This is your civic duty. You owe it to all of us in this nation. We await your verdict. This court is adjourned.

Bailiff: This court is adjourned. All rise!

*Exit Judge Deborah.*

*The jury retires to the sequestration chamber. The bailiff and everyone else leave the courtroom.*

*Everyone will await further instructions from the judge.*

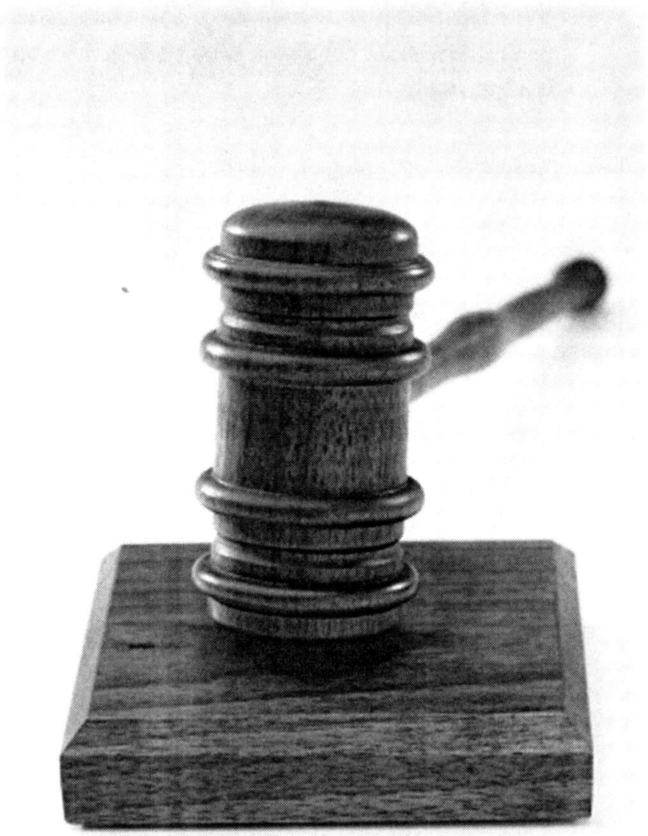

# Scene 11

# The Verdict is In

Judge: Will the defendant King Herod, please stand. *[King Herod rises to his feet. His demeanor is stoic; he passes his right hand through his hair. He looks intently at the judge.]*

Judge: Forewoman of the Jury, please rise.

*[The Forewoman of the Jury stands and turns to the judge.]*

Judge: Forewoman of the Jury, has this jury agreed upon a verdict?

Forewoman: Yes, Your Honor.

Judge: Forewoman of the Jury, is that verdict unanimous?

Forewoman: Yes, Your Honor. We are unanimous in our rendition of the verdict.

Judge: Members of the jury, you have heard that this verdict is a unanimous verdict, what say each of you?

Jury: Yea, Your Honor, the verdict is unanimous, so say we all.

Judge: Forewoman of the Jury, read out the verdict? *[King Herod stands expressionless, as he waits to hear the verdict. There is a profound silence in the courtroom. No one moves or speaks. One could hear a pin drop. All eyes are fixed on the Forewoman of the jury.]*

Forewoman: Your Honor, we the jury find the defendant guilty on all counts.

Count #1: Lies and deception. GUILTY.

Count #2: Denying the birth of Jesus, the Messiah, and King of the Jews. GUILTY.

Count #3: Attempted murder of the Child Jesus, the Messiah and King of the Jews. GUILTY.

Count #4: Crimes against humanity. King Herod ordered the massacre of all the boys two years old or under, in and around Bethlehem. GUILTY

*[King Herod, shows little emotion, he bites his lips, pouts his mouth, and his eyebrows move up and down.]*

Judge: Do you have anything to say, King Herod?

King Herod: Not fair! Not Fair! Where is the justice? When will somebody fix this judicial system? Justice has been denied today. I was deceived by the wise men, and now I am deceived by this court. [With his hands lifted towards heaven] I am innocent of the charges against me. This is a conspiracy to frame me for crimes I did not commit. I am truly innocent of the charges.

Release me and let me go. I fully intend to appeal this verdict, and clear my name someday.

Judge: Enough of your ranting and raving, King Herod. This jury found you guilty on all four counts. Bailiff, handcuff King Herod and lead him out of the door until the time of sentencing. Take him away at once!

*[The Bailiff handcuffs the King, escorts the convicted criminal out of the courtroom, and hands him over to the Marshal to be locked up in the prison. The Bailiff returns to the courtroom.]*

Judge: Thank you jury. Today you have fulfilled your duty to this nation. This court is adjourned until sentencing.

Bailiff: This court is adjourned. All rise!!!

*Exit Judge Deborah,
Every one else follows . . .*

# [SENTENCING DAY HAS ARRIVED]

Judge: Will the defendant King Herod, please stand! [*King Herod picks himself up slowly. He is shaking and the depth of his anxiety is very noticeable.*] [*Sternly*] King Herod, this court must send a strong message to everyone, including you, King Herod, that all those who perpetrate these kinds of crimes against humanity, will face the whole arm of the law. The sentence you will be handed today, King Herod, will serve to deter others who have the same inclinations as you.

Judge: King Herod come forward! [*King Herod moves forward. He looks gaunt and distressed, he bows his head and stares at the floor*] LOOK AT ME, KING HEROD, THE GREAT! For the guilty verdict on all four counts of felony, and through the powers invested in me by the Kingdom, I hereby sentence you to be cast in the extreme outer darkness where you will wail, and weep, and gnash your teeth forever.

King Herod: [interrupting] No, Your Honor, this sentence is just too severe. It is more than I can bear. What would the other people out there think of me? My reputation is forever tarnished. Throughout all of history, no one will have anything favorable to say about me. They will always refer to me as the killer of HOLY INNOCENCE. Please accept my plea bargain as I throw myself on the mercy of this court. [*The King gets down on his knees*] Couldn't you have imposed a lighter sentence on the King? [*He cups his face into his hands and cries aloud, then moans and groans.*]

Judge: [To the Bailiff] Lift him up and take him away! Get this convicted felon out of here, right now! [*King Herod is led away in handcuffs and leg irons.*]

Bailiff: All rise!

*Exit Judge Deborah.*

*Everyone else follows, except the Prosecutor. She spends a brief moment savouring the taste of her victory that put King Herod away for life. Then she vacates the courtroom wheeling her very bulky briefcase behind her. Oblivious to the fact that The PRESS was waiting for her outside the courthouse, she continues on with great delight leaving the courtroom behind her.*

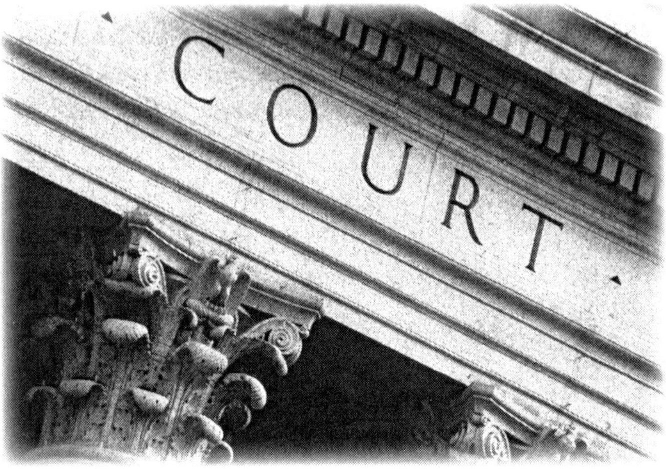
COURT

# Outside of the Courtroom

*[Members of the Press are in hot pursuit of the Prosecutor, Madam G. Louisburg.]*

The Press: Madam Prosecutor, my name is Cemonde, and I am here from the TV Station GYP. "My question to you is this, "What are your thoughts on the verdict as rendered by the Jury?"

Prosecutor: I think it was the correct verdict. The jury convicted him on all four charges. Did they not?

The Press: Madame Prosecutor, my name is Albertina, and I am here from TV Station HJTI. "My question to you is this, "What are your thoughts about the sentence? Do you think King Herod received a just sentence?"

Prosecutor: I totally agree with Judge Deborah. I think the sentence was adequate, and just. In giving the maximum sentence, Judge Deborah is sending out a message to others who would be thinking of killing innocent babies in order to fulfill their crooked ambitions, that this Court will not be lenient with them. We are here to protect innocent lives. Period. King Herod will be out of this earth and into the outer darkness for the rest of his life, and beyond. That is where he ought to be. For his crimes he will weep and gnash his teeth for the rest of his life. It is a sentence fitting the crimes.

The Press: Madam Prosecutor, my name is Anisha and I am from TV station WTQR. My question to you is this, "In the future, do you plan taking on more cases of this nature?"

Prosecutor: Yes, I am ready to perform this public service at any time. Bringing a criminal to justice is my job, and I take my job very seriously.

The Press: Thank you, Madam Prosecutor for finding the time to share your feelings on this case with members of the Press.

Prosecutor: Thank you all, and have a good day!

## ENTER JESUS.

*[He meets the people where they are; milling around outside the courthouse and pondering the events of the trial.]*

# Scene 12

# The Grand Finale

Jesus: Thank you, my friends for your great witness. Keep up your faith in the Living God and in me. Here are some words of encouragement that I want to leave with you today.

1. My friends, blessed are your eyes, for they see, and your ears, for they hear. Truly, I tell you, many prophets and righteous people longed to see what you see, but did not see it, and longed to hear what you hear, but did not hear it. *(Matthew 13:16)*

2. I came to set you free. I came that you might have life and have it more abundantly. (John 10:10)

3. Blessed are you when people revile you and persecute you and utter all kinds of evil against you falsely, on my account. Rejoice and be glad for your reward is great in heaven, for in the same way they persecuted the prophets who were before you. (Matthew 5: 11-12)

4. You have heard that it was said to those of ancient times. "You shall not murder; and whoever murders shall be liable to judgment." But I say to you that if you are angry with a brother or sister you will be liable to judgment; and if you insult a brother or sister, you will be liable to the council; and if you say, "You fool," you will be liable to the hell of fire. (Matthew 5:21-22)

5. Love one another as I have loved you. By this may all people know that you are my disciples; if you have love one for another. And because of the increase of lawlessness, the love of many will grow cold. But the one who endures to the end will be saved. And this good news of the kingdom will be proclaimed throughout the world as a testimony to all the nations; and then the end will come. (Matthew 24: 12-14)

6. My love for you is so great. I divested myself of my Godhead, taking the form of a slave, being born in human likeness. And being found in human form, I humbled myself and became obedient to the point of death, even death on the cross. (Philippians 2: 6-8) I came to save you. I did not remain a baby in the manger. I grew up and the grace of God was upon me. Today, I offer that same grace of God to all of you.

FAREWELL. GOD LOVES YOU ALL!

*Jesus walks away and the crowd disperses.*

# CONCLUSION

The pursuit to which I am intensely devoted is a passion for Jesus and the spiritual life. I will continue to research, and reflect on the Biblical stories that gave me a grand perspective of my Scriptural heritage.

I am grateful to the men and women I sought to portray in The Mystery of the Nativity of Jesus. They have all in some way contributed to my understanding of the events that took place in Israel two thousand years ago.

I am especially grateful to the mothers whose pain, grief, and frustration I tried to capture in this drama. For them it was no joke; rather it was real pain, real grief, and real frustration. On their behalf, I am tremendously grateful that they had their day in court to tell their story and gain justice for themselves. Because of this drama, I say, "Justice was done, in spite of the fact that it was only a fictitious trial."

CPSIA information can be obtained at www.ICGtesting.com
Printed in the USA
LVOW102047131112
307173LV00001B/2/P